Contents

Assembly Today for Key Stage 2

INTRODUCTION

Coming up with new and interesting ideas for assembly can often be an extremely difficult and time consuming task. Ideally, of course, the subject matter should have a clear moral message, should be motivating to the pupils and be of a broadly Christian outlook. In this book we have created a range of assemblies for use within a wide range of schools and appropriate for all children regardless of their faith or cultural heritage.

The assemblies in this book are arranged according to appropriate times of year, although many can be used across the whole school year as well. Each assembly has a moral or appropriate message, a visual or physical element, a prayer and a suggested song or hymn.

For most of the assemblies you will need to use an overhead projector. Where the assemblies include stories we have sometimes provided silhouettes that need to be photocopied on to paper and then cut out (before the assembly) for display on the OHP – this creates the simplest form of shadow puppet show that is certain to gain the childrens' full attention! For other stories a separate picture is provided that can be photocopied on to acetate and placed on the OHP to act as a visual aid while the story is being read out. For the rest of the stories we have mixed the pictures with the text. Here you can photocopy on to acetate sheets and then present the story on OHP so the children can follow the text as well as the pictures. If you have plenty of preparation time you could involve children in the re-tellng of the story or they could even role play the issues being addressed.

For some of the assemblies you might want to simply follow the script that is provided on the teachers' page while for others you might want to read the assembly first and then present it in your own words. The script in italic type can be used directly or use it as the basis for your presentation. Whatever style of presentation you choose, assemblies should be enjoyable and thought-provoking experiences for all concerned.

Andrew Brodie: Assembly Today KS2 © A&C Black Publishers Ltd. 2005

Big fish and little fish

 AIM: To value one's individual qualities without needing to feel important.

PREPARATION

- If you are planning to use an overhead projector, photocopy 'Big fish and little fish' (page 4) on to acetate or you may prefer to make an enlarged version on bigger paper.

INTRODUCTION

Ask children to indicate by a show of hands whether they would like to be famous. Next ask if anyone can think of reasons why it might be better not to be well known. Accept and discuss responses.

MAIN ACTIVITY

Today we are going to look at one of Aesop's fables.

Present the story by reading it to the pupils whilst also showing it on the OHP, and/or display an enlarged copy of the story.

What do you think the moral of that story was? Accept responses – hopefully someone will offer the opinion that sometimes it is better to be insignificant.

REFLECTION

Many people fall into the trap of wanting to be famous or important in some way, but very often it is easier to live a happy and fulfilled life without any of the trappings of 'fame and fortune'.

Does God know famous people any better than he knows any other people?

Accept responses and help pupils to consider that God sees the way they live their lives, i.e. God knows everyone, not only those who are well known within human society.

Prayer

Dear God,
Thank you for making us all as individuals with a range of talents and abilities. Thank you too for watching over each one of us every day. Help us to learn that it is not important to be rich or famous, but that it is the way we live our lives each day that truly matters. Amen

Song

This little light of mine   (Alleluya, 14: *A&C Black*)

Big fish and little fish

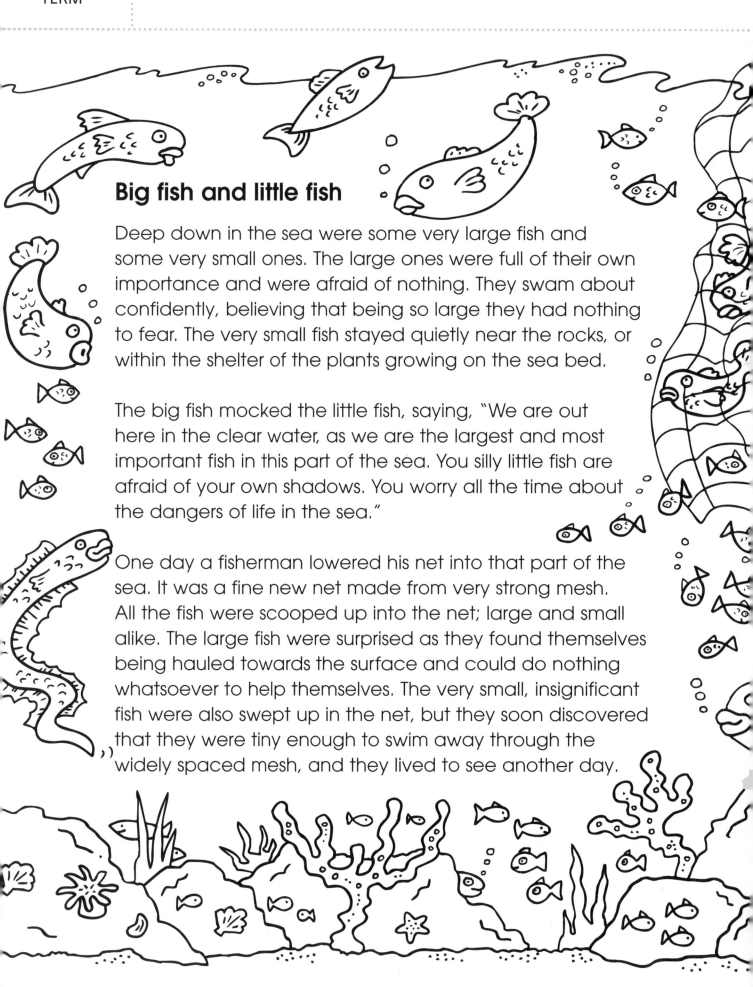

Big fish and little fish

Deep down in the sea were some very large fish and some very small ones. The large ones were full of their own importance and were afraid of nothing. They swam about confidently, believing that being so large they had nothing to fear. The very small fish stayed quietly near the rocks, or within the shelter of the plants growing on the sea bed.

The big fish mocked the little fish, saying, "We are out here in the clear water, as we are the largest and most important fish in this part of the sea. You silly little fish are afraid of your own shadows. You worry all the time about the dangers of life in the sea."

One day a fisherman lowered his net into that part of the sea. It was a fine new net made from very strong mesh. All the fish were scooped up into the net; large and small alike. The large fish were surprised as they found themselves being hauled towards the surface and could do nothing whatsoever to help themselves. The very small, insignificant fish were also swept up in the net, but they soon discovered that they were tiny enough to swim away through the widely spaced mesh, and they lived to see another day.

Andrew Brodie: Assembly Today KS2 © A&C Black Publishers Ltd. 2005

The enchanted fish

 AIM: To recognise the difference between need and greed.

PREPARATION

■ Photocopy and cut out the silhouettes from 'The enchanted fish' (page 6).

INTRODUCTION

Today's story is about a fish and it is based on a traditional tale. The story is designed to make you think about what we really need and what is just greed.

STORY

There was once a poor fisherman who lived with his wife in a hut near the river. (Place hut on OHP.) One day the fisherman caught the finest fish he had ever seen. He was just about to land it when, to his surprise, the fish spoke.

"Please don't kill and eat me," said the fish, "for I am an enchanted fish."

The fisherman was amazed and allowed the fish to swim away. When he returned home he told his wife about the enchanted fish.

"You stupid man," said his wife, "if the fish was enchanted why didn't you ask it to give us something in return for its freedom? We could have had a fine new house with a little garden where I could have grown fine fresh vegetables for us. Go down to the river this minute and call him. Perhaps even now he will help us."

So back went the man and called to the fish. A few moments later the enchanted fish appeared. The man explained that his wife would like a new house, and when the man returned home, there was a fine new house with a little garden for growing vegetables. (Remove hut from OHP and replace it with the house.)

For the next few weeks everything seemed wonderful. Then one evening, the man noticed his wife was rather quiet. "Are you all right dear?" he asked.

"No," came the reply, "We should have asked for a mansion with servants to do all the work. Go back and tell that fish of yours that we need a mansion." The man was not happy, but he returned to the river and called to the fish as his wife had asked. He explained that his wife felt that a mansion with servants would make her life easier.

"Go home to your mansion," said the fish kindly. Sure enough when the man returned home there was a very grand mansion, complete with servants. (Replace house with mansion on OHP.) Needless to say his wife was delighted. Life was peaceful for a while until the man's wife became discontented again. "Whatever is wrong dear?" he asked.

"I'll tell you what's wrong," she replied. "We only have a mansion, whilst further along the river I have seen a grand castle. Go and see that fish and tell him I want a castle to live in." The man was very unhappy about this, but that evening he went back down to the river and called the enchanted fish. The fish appeared almost immediately, and the man explained the problem. The fish thought for a moment, then said, "Go home and your wife will have been given the home she deserves."

The man returned home to find his wife sitting crying outside the hut they had started off in. (Swap mansion for hut.) "Whatever have you done husband?" she asked.

"Only what you asked me to he replied. The fish said he would give you the home you deserved, and I think he has."

REFLECTION

What do you think is the lesson we might all take from that story?

Accept and discuss responses.

Prayer

Dear God,
Please help us to know the difference between genuine needs and selfish greed.
Give us the strength to work each day with a caring sharing attitude.   *Amen*

Song   Sing Hosanna   (*Alleluya, 3: A&C Black*)

The enchanted fish

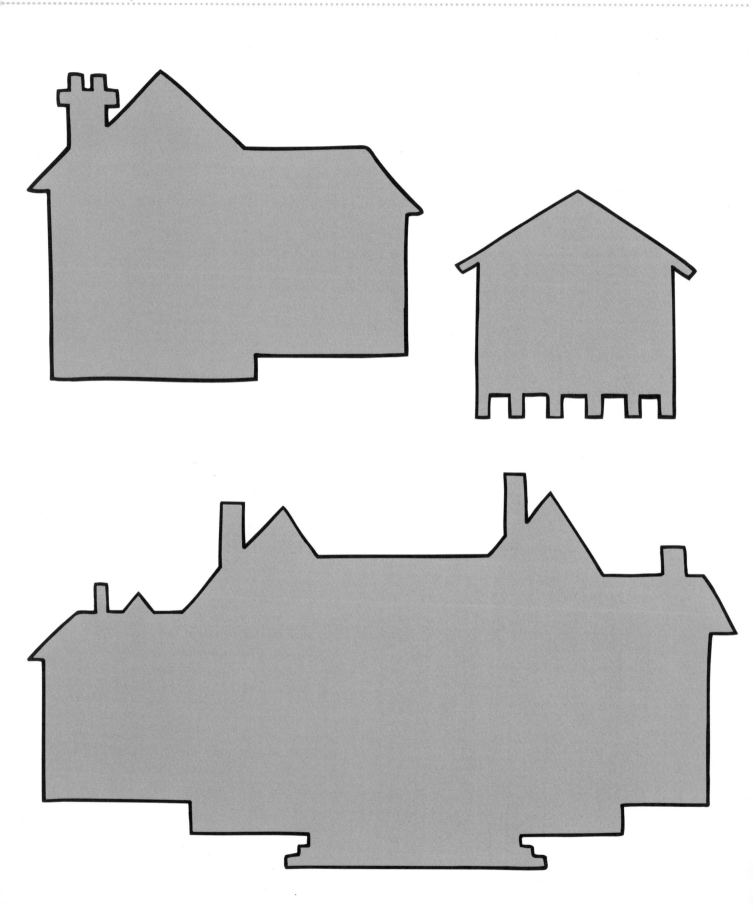

Desert island

AIM: To encourage children to realise how dependent we are on each other.

PREPARATION

- Photocopy the 'Desert island' (page 8) on to acetate ready to place on the OHP.

INTRODUCTION

Have you ever read a book about a desert island? Or perhaps you have seen a film about someone who is stuck on a desert island.

ACTIVITY

I know some books about desert islands: 'Robinson Crusoe' by Daniel Defoe is a very old book. It's about a man called Robinson Crusoe who works on a ship that gets caught in a very violent storm. The ship gets wrecked and Robinson is the only person who survives. He gets washed up on an island. We call it a 'desert island' because it is deserted – in other words, no one else lives there. Robinson Crusoe lives on his island for years; he grows a long beard and he has to make his own clothes. (Place the illustration on the OHP.) *Eventually he finds another man there; he finds him on a Friday so do you know what he calls him? Man Friday.*

Another book about a desert island is 'Kensuke's Kingdom' by Michael Morpurgo. In this story a boy called Michael gets knocked off his parents' boat into the sea. His parents don't even know he is gone until it is too late to find him. The waves carry him to an island where he is rescued by a very old man who looks after him.

I sometimes think it would be lovely to be alone on a desert island, especially one where the sun shines and the sea is blue. What do you think? Would you like to be alone on a desert island? What would be the good things about it? When I raise my arm I would like you to talk to the person next to you for one minute. Not yet, wait for the arm. See if you can come up with two good things about living on an island. At the end of the minute, I will lower my arm and, even if you are not ready, see if you can stop talking at exactly that moment so we can hear some of the ideas.

Did you think of two good things? I will ask just a few people to tell me what their two good things are.

But sometimes, I think that I would not like to live on a desert island. I can think of lots of bad things about it, can you? Let's try the raising and lowering of my arm again. You have one minute to think of two bad things about living alone on an island.

Did you think of two bad things?

REFLECTION

I am glad that I am not alone on a desert island. I am not frightened and I am not afraid of the dark. I have enough food and I have enough water. But the most special thing is that I am lucky to have my friends and family about me. They help me sometimes and I help them sometimes.

Prayer

Dear God,
Thank you for our friends and families. Thank you for all the people around us who help us. Help us to help each other whenever we can. Help us not to be lonely and not to let other people feel lonely. Amen

Song   Look out for loneliness   (Someone's Singing, Lord 36: *A&C Black*)

Desert island

Putting the interests of others before your own

 AIM: To encourage the children to think about putting the needs of other people before themselves.

PREPARATION

■ Photocopy the pictures from 'Putting the interests of others before your own' (page 10) on to acetate and cut out the separate people.

▦ INTRODUCTION

I would like you to think about what the following people have in common. Listen (and watch) carefully as some of them are 'named' famous people and some are types of people. (As each character is read out place the appropriate picture on the OHP.)

Florence Nightingale	*Grace Darling*	*Life boat crews*
Fire fighters	*Mary Seacole*	

Now invite ideas as to the common element of the characters shown. Hopefully someone will realise that these people all have on occasion put the needs of others before their own. Briefly discuss each of the characters and in what way they put the needs of others first. You could say something like:

Life boat crew risk their own lives to save those in difficulties at sea.
Fire fighters risk their lives when entering burning buildings to save others.
Grace Darling helped her father (who was the keeper of the Longstone Lighthouse) to row out and save people clinging to the wreck of the Forfarshire, in heavy seas, in 1838. This clearly put her own life at risk.
Mary Seacole and Florence Nightingale risked their own health and lives to nurse soldiers in the Crimean war in the 1850s.

Point out that these examples feature people who are (or have been) in situations where they not only have put the lives of others before their own, but that the people saved were or are not personally known by their rescuers.
Ask pupils if they know of any other people or types of job that have resulted in putting their own health, or even life, at risk to keep others safe and well.
Accept and discuss responses – these may of course be related to topical events covered in the media.
Consider with pupils what type of people allow themselves to be put into these situations. Look for responses to include ordinary people who care about others – people with courage that may or may not be evident in the normal course of life.

▦ REFLECTION

None of us ever know when our own courage and inner strength could be tested. Often exceptional and unexpected events enable people to display strength of character they did not know they possessed.

Prayer

Dear God,
We give you thanks for the courage that you have given to us. Help us to be strong enough to use our bravery wisely and well. Thank you for the people who regularly put the needs of others before their own in their day to day lives, jobs or voluntary work. Amen

Song   Guantanamera   (Alleluya, 11: *A&C Black*)

Putting the interests of others before your own

Andrew Brodie: Assembly Today KS2 © A&C Black Publishers Ltd. 2005

The widow's coins

 AIM: For pupils to understand the role of 'giving' within the community and that their own contributions can be important.

> **PREPARATION**
>
> ■ Photocopy the 'The widow's coins' story (page 12) on to an OHP transparency.

INTRODUCTION

Ask pupils to name some recent charity events/appeals that they know of. Accept and discuss responses.

You may, if appropriate, ask if any pupils would like to share information about which they helped with or contributed to and how they did this. You are looking for broad statements not financial amounts. Their contributions might be in kind not cash and the importance of giving time and talents should be emphasised too.

ACTIVITY

Many families give a regular donation to help with the running of their religious faith.

Today we are going to hear a story from the Christian bible. Whatever religion you and your family belong to, this story is interesting as it encourages us all to think about our giving. Not just within our own churches but on the many occasions when we might feel it is important to try and help with a worthy cause.

Read and display the story on the accompanying sheet.

After reading the story leave it on display and ask pupils what lesson they think is in the story. Hopefully they will have realised that it is about valuing not the amount but the personal sacrifice involved.

REFLECTION

Ask pupils how thinking about this story might have any impact on their lives. Use the responses to this to encourage pupils to be willing to give up something when they feel it is important to give to a good cause, e.g. pupils could be prepared to give up sweets for a week to give to a charity event. If there is a collection for a worthwhile cause, giving what they can of their own (with of course their parents' permission) is better than just expecting a parental contribution.

Point out that although the story is about giving money, there are many other ways to give: time, effort, encouragement, support and so on.

Prayer

Dear God,

Help us to think about ways we can improve the world by our own generosity. Give us the strength we may need to give cheerfully to help others, particularly when this may mean going without something ourselves. Thank you for giving us open minds, loving hearts and the ability to help those around us. Amen

Song

God loves a cheerful giver   (Alleluya, 2: *A&C Black*)
or
Guantanamera   (Alleluya, 11: *A&C Black*)

The widow's coins

The widow's coins

Jesus was in the temple one day and he saw many rich people putting large offerings into the collection. As he watched he noticed a poor widow going towards the collection box. When she reached it she dropped in just two small coins.

On seeing this, Jesus said to his disciples, "That poor woman put more into the collection box than all the others. They are all rich and had plenty to spare, but she, being so very poor, gave all that she had."

Beethoven and Braille

AIM: To encourage pupils to value their senses and to appreciate the strength and courage of those whose senses fail.

PREPARATION

- Photocopy the Braille alphabet (page 14) onto an OHP transparency.
- Find some music by Beethoven to play to the pupils, preferably the ninth symphony.

INTRODUCTION

Can you tell me what our senses are? Can you identify them? Encourage children to give responses including touch, sight, hearing, taste and smell. *Not everyone has all their senses. We are fortunate if we can see clearly, if we can hear clearly, if we can smell and taste our food and if we can touch things and pick them up.*

Which, do you think, is the most important sense?

Which, do you think, would be the most important sense to a musician?

Children may make suggestions such as 'sight', so that the musician can read the music, 'touch' so that the musician can feel the musical instrument and 'hearing' so that the musician can hear the sound of the music.

ACTIVITY

One of the most famous musicians ever to have lived was called Ludwig van Beethoven. He was born in 1770 and even as a child he showed great talent with music. Though one of his teachers did say that he was 'hopeless' as a musician! When he was still quite a young man Beethoven began to lose his hearing. He was still able to write marvellous music and some of his greatest music was written after he became deaf. Listen to this piece of music. (Play a part of the ninth symphony.)

Now I am going to tell you about somebody who was blind. His name was Louis Braille. He wasn't blind when he was born but when he was a very little boy he became blind after an accident. When he grew up Louis Braille invented a way of showing the alphabet for blind people. We can see what that alphabet looks like but, of course, blind people can't. Show the Braille alphabet on the screen. *We call this the Braille alphabet. How do you think that blind people can read Braille?* Encourage responses that produce the answer 'by touching' or 'by feeling'. *Yes, the dots are raised up so that the blind people can feel them. Just like we learn to read in school, blind people learn to read the dots just by feeling them with their fingers. Sometimes whole books are written in Braille and blind people can read them by feeling the dots on the pages. Can you read these two words that are written in Braille?* Allow time for the children to work out that the two words say 'thank you'.

REFLECTION

We have heard about two special people who had disabilities: Beethoven who became deaf and Braille who became blind. Let's give thanks for their lives and also for our senses.

Prayer

Dear God,

We thank you for the lives of Beethoven and Braille. Beethoven who gave the world great music and Braille who gave the world an alphabet for blind people. We thank you also for our senses: touch, hearing, sight, taste and smell. Help us to have the strength to use our senses well. *Amen*

Song   He gave me eyes so I could see   (Someone's Singing, Lord 19: *A&C Black*)

Beethoven and Braille

The Braille Alphabet

A   B   C   D   E   F   G   H   I   J

K   L   M   N   O   P   Q   R   S   T

U   V   W   X   Y   Z   and the

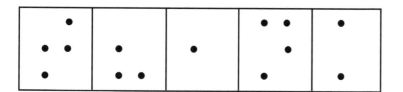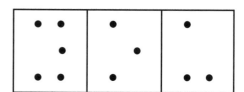

The importance of honesty

 AIM: To consider the importance of honesty (a valued quality in all major religions and cultures).

> **PREPARATION**
> ■ Photocopy the 'The importance of honesty' story (page 16) on to an OHP transparency.

▣ INTRODUCTION

Today we are going to think about the importance of being honest.
Would anyone like to tell us why you think it is important to be honest? Accept responses.
Are there any occasions when it might be difficult to be honest? Accept responses.

We are going to hear a very well known fable by Aesop that may help us think a bit more about the possible consequences of dishonesty.

▣ MAIN ACTIVITY

Either – read the given fable and use an enlarged photocopied version for display later
Or – show the fable on an overhead projector so that pupils can see it as it is being read to them.

▣ REFLECTION

What do you think the lesson is in that story? Hope for responses concerning a liar not being believed, even on occasions when he/she may be speaking the truth.
That tale is very well known and you might think not at all to do with you and the way you live your lives – none of you are left alone to guard flocks of sheep against wolves! There may however have been times when you may have found it convenient not to be completely truthful. Perhaps you might have got into the habit of letting a little brother or sister take the blame for something you have done for instance!

If appropriate here, and if time allows, you may wish to ask pupils to share any examples of occasions when dishonesty has prevailed in their lives. Make it clear that this is not a time to point out the faults of others!

Prayer

Dear God,
Please give us the wisdom and courage to be truthful in our daily lives. Help us to remember the importance of honest words and honest actions as we journey through each day.   *Amen*

Song

This little light of mine   (Alleluya, 14: *A&C Black*)
or
This train is bound for Glory   (Alleluya, 25: *A&C Black*)

The importance of honesty

The Boy Who Cried Wolf

A young shepherd boy was often left alone to protect the farmer's flock of sheep. At first he was quite happy to watch the sheep carefully and took great pride in completing his task well. After a while though he began to find his job boring. There was no one else to talk to or play with, and he couldn't teach sheep to do tricks to pass the time.

One day, when he was feeling particularly fed up, he decided to pass the time more enjoyably by playing what he thought was a harmless trick. When all the sheep were grazing peacefully the boy started to yell as loudly as he could, "HELP! HELP! THERE'S A WOLF! HELP! WOLF, WOLF!" His cries could be heard by the men in the surrounding fields and even by those in the nearest village. Within minutes they were running towards him from all directions to save the sheep. It soon became clear that there was no sign of a wolf anywhere about and the men were very cross as they went back to their jobs and their homes.

For a few weeks the boy remembered the trouble his trick had caused and each day he guarded his flock with care. Then one day the sun was hot and the day seemed to go on forever. Whatever could he do to liven up the day? He had so enjoyed his previous trick that he decided to do it again. He knew he would be in trouble, but he thought it was worth it to see all the men come puffing up the hill towards him. So again he yelled as loudly as he possibly could, "WOLF! WOLF! HELP ME! WOLF, WOLF, WOLF!"

Again the men came rushing up the hill, and again it soon became obvious that there was no wolf anywhere about. The boy was in trouble yet again, and the men returned to their jobs and homes grumbling about the shepherd boy's stupidity.

The very next week as the sun was nearly setting the boy saw signs of movement in some trees near the edge of the field. The sheep seemed edgy and all came towards him bleating anxiously. Instantly the boy looked all around, he had an uncomfortable feeling that something was wrong but he simply didn't know what. His apprehension turned to fear when he saw a large grey wolf appearing from between the trees eying up the nearest of the flock. The shepherd boy's desperate cries could be heard for miles around: "HELP! WOLF, WOLF, WOLF!" No one appeared so the boy screamed again until he felt his lungs would burst, 'WOLF, WOLF, WOLF!"

While the shepherd boy sank to the floor sobbing, and the village folk grumbled about 'that silly boy playing tricks again', the wolf was enjoying a delicious meal of tender lamb.

Andrew Brodie: Assembly Today KS2 © A&C Black Publishers Ltd. 2005

Compassionate honesty

 AIM: To promote compassion in our dealings with those around us.

PREPARATION

■ If time allows, a little forward planning for this assembly would enable you get the most out of the time by dealing with the given scenarios as role plays rather than just questions and answers.

INTRODUCTION

We all recognise the importance of honesty, even though it is not always easy to tell the truth. We also all recognise the importance of trying never to hurt the feelings of others when talking to them. Our assembly today will look as some situations in which being truthful and being kind can be particularly difficult.

MAIN ACTIVITY

We are going to begin by thinking about two situations that can be difficult to deal with in a way that is sensitive to the feelings of others while still being honest.

You are given a birthday present by a caring relative – it is an item of clothing that you do not like. The relative is there when you open the present and is looking expectantly at you for your reaction. How should you respond?

Consider with the pupils the hurt that could be caused by brutal honesty. You may wish to encourage comments about favourable aspects of the garment, e.g. the colour, or its suitability for wearing at a particular type of event. These would be honest without causing offence.

A friend has had a hair cut. In your opinion the new style does not suit them but it would be impossible to pretend that you have not noticed the change in their appearance. What might you say so you did not cause offence?

This is another event that is quite likely to happen to pupils. In this instance too, careful honesty should be encouraged. Pupils may give appropriate suggestions such as commenting on the quality of the cut, or asking (in a positive tone) if the other child is delighted with their new look.

If there is time you may wish to ask children to volunteer any other 'honesty dilemma' situations they may have encountered, and discuss how these might be dealt with.

REFLECTION

Life is full of situations where we have to consider carefully how we should do the right thing. Often it is best to think for a moment before speaking as once words have come out of your mouth they can never be put back again! A few words that take just a moment to utter may cause a hurt for a very long time.

Prayer

Dear God,
Grant us the wisdom to use our honesty in a caring way. Help us not to harm others with thoughtless words or deeds. Give us the words and actions that will help those around us to retain their dignity and self-respect. *Amen*

Song   This little light of mine   (Alleluya, 14: *A&C Black*)

Stone soup

AIM: To encourage children to realise that there are some people in the world who will be willing to cheat or trick them and, although they should try to be kind they should also be careful.

PREPARATION

■ Photocopy the silhouettes from page 19 on to card then cut them out ready for use at appropriate parts of the story.

INTRODUCTION

Most people in the world are very kind. Most people like to get on well with others. Most people don't hurt other people. Most people are quite good at sharing. But there are a few people who may try to trick you. There are a few people who you can't trust.

STORY

One day a young man was wandering along the road and he realised that he was feeling very hungry. Just then, he came across an old lady who was busy working in her garden. He leaned over her garden wall and said in a friendly sort of way, "Hello, you're working hard."

The old lady stretched herself up, holding on to her back because it was aching from all the hard work that she had done. "Hello," she replied. "Yes, it is hard work but I do enjoy it. I like to grow my own vegetables because they are so expensive in the shops." (Place picture of old lady on OHP.)

"I love vegetables," said the young man, "especially fresh ones."

"Well, I am afraid I can't spare any," said the old lady, "I need all these to last me through the winter. I can't even afford to pick any for my dinner today."

The young man looked carefully at the lady's garden. There were lots of vegetables growing there: carrots, potatoes, leeks, swedes. He looked carefully at the lady's house. It was a very smart house with tidy curtains at the windows and a shining front door. There was also a very smart car in the drive. He thought that the old lady was a bit mean, saying she couldn't spare any vegetables.

"Would you like me to cook your dinner for you?" asked the young man.

"I've just told you I can't afford to pick any vegetables for my dinner."

"Don't worry," said the young man, "I can make a marvellous dinner from this magic stone that I carry with me," and he produced from his pocket a lovely round pebble that was coloured white with red streaks running through it. (Place picture of young man with stone on OHP and remove old lady.)

The old lady laughed. "You can't cook dinner from a stone!" she exclaimed.

"Watch me and I'll prove it,' returned the young man, with a big friendly smile on his face.

"Come on in then," said the old lady, quite excited at the thought that she might be getting dinner for nothing. She hurried into the house and the young man followed her through to the kitchen. It was a large kitchen with lots of bright, shining pots and pans. The young man selected a large saucepan. (Add saucepan to young man picture.) *He half-filled it with some water then placed it on the cooker to start heating the water. He used a spoon to lower the stone carefully into the water. Very soon the water started to boil.*

"Umm, that smells good," said the young man. "This is going to be the best soup ever!" The old lady looked on in amazement.

"Yes, marvellous," added the young man, "mind you, it would be even better with one or two potatoes in it."

The old lady thought for a moment, then said, "I have got one or two potatoes we could put in."

"Excellent," said the young man as he chopped up the potatoes. "I love this soup. I like it with carrots in it but we haven't got any carrots."

"Yes I have," called the old lady and she rushed out to the garden to pull up four fat carrots. (Put old lady back on the OHP.)

"Wonderful," said the young man as he chopped up the carrots and tipped them into the saucepan. "This soup is going to be perfect. Well, nearly perfect. It would be great with some leeks in but still, never mind."

"Oh, I've got lots of leeks," said the old lady and was soon back with an armful of leeks.

"Exquisite," said the young man. "It's nearly ready. It would be nice to have bread with it but I know you can't afford bread so we'll have it just as it is."

"Well, I can afford a little bit of bread," said the old lady, producing a large crusty loaf and laying the table with two places.

Very soon the young man and the old lady sat down to their meal.

"Marvellous!" said the young man.

"Gorgeous!" said the old lady.

"Excellent!" said the young man.

"Perfect!" said the old lady.

"Fantastic!" said the young man.

"Just to think that you made this lovely meal from a stone," said the old lady.

"It's amazing."

After they had finished their dinner they sat and enjoyed a cup of tea together then the young man said that it was time for him to go.

"Thank you for having me," he said, politely, "you were very kind."

"No, you were the one who was kind," the old lady replied. "Please come again one day."

After the young man had left the old lady tidied up the kitchen. "I haven't got much bread left," she said to herself. "Come to think of it, I haven't many potatoes or carrots or leeks."

▦ REFLECTION

There are several questions that you may like to put to the children:

What did the young man make the soup from?

Who was mean in this story?

Who tricked whom?

Was the young man a nice person?

Was the old lady a nice person?

Who could we trust in this story? Could we trust both people?

Could we trust either of them?

Who was greedy? The children could point out that both people were greedy because they both wanted something for nothing.

In what way was the old lady very silly? There could be several answers to this question but the one that should be stressed is that the old lady should not have let a stranger into her house.

Although we should try to be polite to people we meet we should always be careful because, unfortunately, there are some people that we cannot trust. The old lady in the story was safe because the young man was not dangerous but he could have been and she should have been more careful. Of course, she was being greedy too because she wanted something for nothing; she should have been less selfish in this way and she should always be more careful with strangers.

Prayer

Dear God,

Please help us to be polite to people we meet but give us also the strength and good sense to avoid dangers from people who we cannot trust.   *Amen*

Song   The journey of life   (Someone's Singing, Lord 28: *A&C Black*)

Stone soup

Oh Christmas tree

 AIM: To use the symbolism of the Christmas tree to encourage children to think about good intentions.

PREPARATION

- Photocopy on to paper, then cut out the silhouette of the Christmas tree on page 22.
- Photocopy the illustration on page 23 on to acetate.
- Gather some coloured whiteboard pens for pupils to use during the assembly.

INTRODUCTION

I wonder how many of you have got Christmas trees at home. Do you know why we bring Christmas trees into our houses?
Some people say that it's because of the shape of the tree. (Put the Christmas tree silhouette on the OHP.) *Look at the picture on the screen – how would you describe the shape of the tree?*
It looks a bit like a triangle and I have heard some Christians say that the triangular shape of the tree represents God the father, Jesus the son and the holy spirit of God. I know other people who say that we bring the tree in to celebrate the green leaves of this type of tree in the winter time when many other trees have lost their leaves. We call trees that keep their leaves, like the Christmas tree, evergreen trees; we call trees that lose their leaves in the winter deciduous trees.

Can you think of another evergreen tree that we bring in at Christmas time? We don't usually bring the whole tree in, just some twigs with leaves and berries on.
So, the Christmas tree could represent the holy trinity of the father, the son or the holy spirit and it could represent life through the fact that its leaves are green. Both of these are good explanations why we bring Christmas trees in. Once we bring them in, of course, we decorate them.

A long time ago in this country, not many people used to bring trees into their houses to decorate. In other parts of Europe Christmas trees were very popular but here they weren't. Then Queen Victoria married a man from Germany, called Prince Albert. Prince Albert liked to have a Christmas tree in the royal palace and because of this it became the fashionable thing to do and soon nearly everybody had a Christmas tree.

ACTIVITY

Today I am going to ask you to help me to decorate a Christmas tree. (Put the illustration of the tree on the screen.) *I am going to ask some people to come out and colour in the baubles on the tree but each bauble must be very special. I would like you to try to think of a special word to show a good intention that we should all have over Christmas time. For example, a special word like 'helping' – we could have the intention of helping at Christmas. See if you can think of a good word then perhaps you can come out and colour the bauble to show this good intention.* Accept responses and invite the individuals to come to the OHP to colour the baubles. Hopefully you will receive ideas such as 'caring', 'loving', 'giving', 'thanking', 'appreciating', 'sharing', 'smiling'.

REFLECTION

As we look at the tree and its coloured baubles let's think about the words we have come up with.

Prayer

Dear God,
Help us to have good intentions at Christmas time. Help us to follow these intentions at Christmas time and throughout the coming year. Amen

Song   Tree of light   (Sing a Christmas Cracker, 3: *A&C Black*)

Oh Christmas tree 1

Oh Christmas tree 2

The Lynmouth lifeboat

 AIM: To raise children's awareness of the dedication of people who work in the rescue services.

PREPARATION

■ Prior to the assembly photocopy the picture from page 25 on to an OHP transparency. Place the picture on the OHP screen after the introduction.

▦ INTRODUCTION

At the moment it's a very dark time of the year. We call this the spring term because spring starts at the end of this term but really it could be called the winter term. It goes dark early in the evening and it stays dark until after we get up in the morning. Sometimes at this time of year we have lots of rain. Now try to imagine what it's like when there's a very bad storm as well. Today I am going to tell you a true story. It happened in January in the year 1899.

▦ STORY

The 12th January 1899 was a very stormy day and a small ship called the Forest Hall was caught in the storm. The crew knew that their ship was in serious danger so they sent out distress signals. The message that a ship was in trouble reached a man called Jack Crowcombe who was the leader of the Lynmouth lifeboat crew. (Put the Lifeboat picture on the OHP screen.)

Jack gathered his crew together and they set out to launch the lifeboat but when they got to the launching ramp they realised that they just couldn't do it – they couldn't even get to the launching ramp because huge waves were crashing against the sea wall. Jack thought hard and concluded that the only way they could launch the lifeboat was to launch it from a different place altogether and the only place that that could be done was the village of Porlock. But Porlock was more than twenty kilometres away over very rough roads. These were determined men. The lifeboatmen lifted the boat on to its carriage and harnessed the horses, then they set off. They knew that the journey would be long and difficult and they soon encountered their first problem: an extremely steep hill to climb. The horses pulled and strained and the men pushed and strained. Half way up the hill a wheel came off so they had to stop to repair it but soon they were on their way again. Once they reached the top of the hill it was easier for a while but then they reached some narrow lanes and discovered that the carriage was too wide to fit through. They lifted the boat off the carriage and pushed it along.

At last the men and boat reached the top of Porlock Hill; now their problem was to hold the boat back as the hill sloped very steeply down to Porlock Bay. They held tightly on to the boat and carefully eased it down the hill. By now they had been working all through the night and it was early morning on 13th January. There in the bay they could see the damaged ship, the Forest Hall.

These were determined men. They managed to launch the lifeboat and with the help of another boat and its crew they attached ropes to the Forest Hall and towed her to safety. They were tired, they were hungry, they were exhausted but they had done it – they had rescued the crew of the Forest Hall.

▦ REFLECTION

Did you notice that I repeated a phrase several times during the story? Do you remember what that phrase was?

Prayer

Dear God,
Thank you for the people of all rescue services who are willing to risk their lives to help others. They set us an example by their determination. Help us to be determined to do good deeds too.   *Amen*

Song

Breton Fisherman's Prayer   (Everyone's Singing, Lord 15: *A&C Black*)

The Lynmouth lifeboat

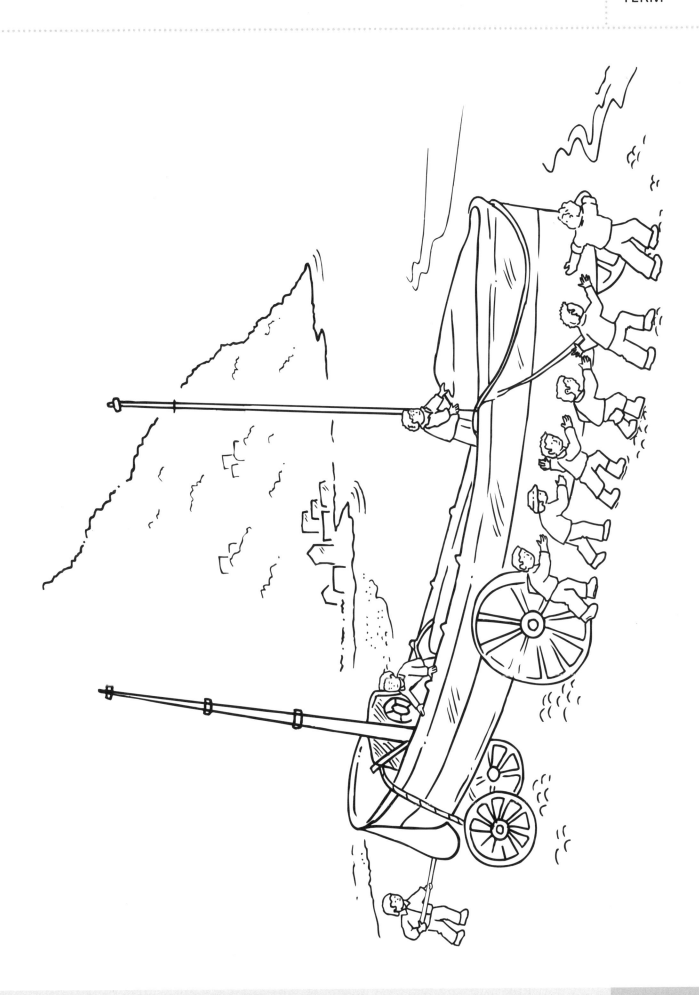

A quiet hero

 AIM: To be aware of one's own strengths and to appreciate those of others.

PREPARATION

■ Photocopy the illustration on page 27 on to an OHP transparency.

▨ INTRODUCTION

Ask the pupils for their definition of the word hero or female equivalent – heroine. Explain that you are going to read a short story about a hero. One who, rather surprisingly perhaps, was young and did not think of himself as either brave or adventurous.

▨ STORY

Many years ago in Holland, there lived a young boy called Eric. He was an ordinary sort of boy; he studied hard at school, he helped his father look after the cattle on their farm and he enjoyed seeing his friends. Eric wasn't especially clever, and he wasn't especially strong. As Eric walked alone to and from school he liked to listen to the waves from the nearby sea as they lapped against the wall of the dam. Often he would climb the sloping sides of the dam walls and stand on the top watching the rippling water. One breezy day in spring when Eric was just nine years old, he was walking home from school when he noticed something he had never seen before. There was a tiny dribble of water dripping down the dam wall. At first Eric just stopped and watched thinking how odd this was. Then he had an uncomfortable feeling that perhaps he should do something about it. After a moment it dawned on him that he must get home as quickly as possible and ask his father for help. It would of course be a real disaster if the sea should break through the wall.

As he turned to head for home he heard a strange pinging sound. Eric looked behind him and, to his horror, he saw that the sea had pushed a tiny stone out of the wall and a steady trickle of water was coming through the newly enlarged hole. Eric panicked for a second. It would take at least twenty minutes for him to get home, and who knows what might happen in that time. Suddenly Eric realised that there was just one thing he could do – he jammed his finger into the small hole. Eric was relieved to see that the flow of water stopped almost immediately. After a few minutes however, his arm began to ache and the finger that was in the wall hurt a lot. Eric wanted to cry, but he didn't; he wanted to run home, but he didn't. He just stood there feeling cold and miserable hoping that help would come soon. He knew that if he didn't stay just where he was, the sea would break through the wall of the dam and many people might lose their lives. It was some hours before Eric's father and brother found him. His brother stayed with him while his father went to get help. The following week there was a huge party held in Eric's honour, and he was treated as a great hero. Even today the act of courage of this one young boy is remembered and every Dutch child grows up hearing the story of the boy who saved Holland.

▨ REFLECTION

This story shows us that it is not always the people that you expect to be heroic that actually are. The amount of noise a person makes in no way indicates what his or her inner strength may prove them capable of. Anyone, maybe one of us, at any time might find ourselves in a situation where we have to act in a courageous way and put the needs of others before our own. I wonder which of us would prove to be a hero – the truth is most people do not find out how brave they might be until an emergency situation occurs.

Prayer

Dear God,
Please help us to have faith in our own strengths. Help us to act in a thoughtful and calm way when dealing with the unexpected events that may happen during our lives. We thank you for giving us opportunities to use our courage to serve the needs of others.   *Amen*

Song

This Little Light of Mine   (Alleluya, 14: *A&C Black*)

          Andrew Brodie: Assembly Today KS2 © A&C Black Publishers Ltd. 2005

A quiet hero

Chinese New Year 1

Aspects of Chinese new year are covered in two assemblies. The first one looks at the facts and traditions, the second concerns the legend of how the years were named.

 AIM: To encourage an interest in the beliefs and traditions of other cultures.

PREPARATION

■ Photocopy page 29 on to an OHP transparency.

▨ INTRODUCTION

Every culture celebrates new year differently, and today we are going to start to think about the Chinese New Year celebrations. Of course as well as in China, people who live all over the world who have Chinese family connections also celebrate in similar ways.

▨ ACTIVITY

Begin by asking pupils for any knowledge of the Chinese New Year that they already have. The extent of this will of course depend on the cultures represented in the school community, and the pupils' previous experiences.

Below you will also find a selection of structured questions to ask. Answers to these questions are on the accompanying information sheet, which is suitable for copying onto acetate for use with an OHP. It can of course also be copied onto paper for display.

What happens on the days leading up to the Chinese new year celebrations?

How are homes decorated for the new year?

What sort of gifts do parents give their children at new year?

How are the years named?

Does anybody know how to say the traditional Chinese – Happy New Year – greeting?

When is Chinese new year?

How is the end of the new year celebration marked?

▨ REFLECTION

It is important that we learn a little about the customs of others and that we respect their customs and traditions.

Prayer

Dear Lord,
Help us to enjoy all the customs and celebrations we share with our families and friends.
Enable us to share in the appreciation of the many festive events enjoyed by others and to learn more about the traditions that are part of cultures other than our own. Amen

Song

Magic Penny   (Alleluya, 10: *A&C Black*)

Chinese New Year information

On the days leading up to the new year every home is thoroughly cleaned. This is to help clean away any of the bad luck from the old year and greet the new year with a fresh start.

Homes are decorated for the new year. The decorations are usually red ones as red symbolizes the colour of good luck.

On the Chinese new year's day children are given presents of money in red envelopes. The envelopes are red to represent good luck.

The cycle of twelve named years are

RAT	1996	OX	1997
TIGER	1998	HARE	1999
DRAGON	2000	SNAKE	2001
HORSE	2002	RAM	2003
MONKEY	2004	COCKEREL	2005
DOG	2006	PIG	2007

The Chinese words pronounced 'Kung Hey Fat Choy' form the traditional Chinese new year greeting.

The traditional Chinese calendar does not begin each year on January 1st. Instead the year starts at the time of the first full moon over China (after the sun enters aquarius) – this is usually between late January and late February. This is why the Chinese new year falls on a different date each (western) year.

At the end of the Chinese New Year, there is what is known as the lantern festival. At this time people take lanterns out into the streets at night and there are fireworks, dragon dancing and playing games.

Chinese New Year 2

 AIM: To encourage an interest in the beliefs and traditions of other cultures.

PREPARATION

- Photocopy the information on page 31 on to an OHP transparency. Please note that the Chinese year is different to the western years and accordingly the year for each animal does not equate exactly with our years; for example, people with birthdays in January may have been born in the year of the animal shown for the previous calendar year.

INTRODUCTION

We have learned a little already about the Chinese New Year. Today we are going to hear the legend of how the twelve years that are named after animals first got their names. Remember even though the story may sound impossible, all our cultures have stories that have been passed down over the years that are equally unlikely to be true.

ACTIVITY

Many years ago, before the years had names, the animals argued about which of them was the most important. To settle this dispute, the gods told the animals to race across the nearby river. They started swimming strongly across the wide river, with the largest and most powerful creatures feeling quite sure that they would win.

The little rat, though an excellent swimmer, soon realised that he was far too small to compete against the biggest of the creatures without using his brain as well as his muscles. By this time the ox had taken the lead, so with a burst of effort the fearless rat managed to catch the ox's tail. From there he climbed up on to its back and enjoyed being carried across the swirling waters. Just as the ox was approaching the river-bank, the rat hopped up to his head and leaped to the shore ahead of him. The ox was most surprised to see such a small creature ahead of him. He just couldn't understand how it could possibly have happened. So the rat won the race and the ox was second, but of course that was not quite the end of the tale, as the other ten animals were still swimming as quickly as they could to reach the river-bank. In third place came the Tiger and fourth place was the hare. Following this the dragon was fifth arriving just before the snake. In seventh place was the horse, followed by the ram and then the monkey. The cockerel came ashore in tenth place, crowing loudly with relief that he was still in one piece. The dog, who was eleventh, shook his furry coat showering the rest with water. Lastly, some considerable time after the other eleven, the pig arrived on the shore. He was disappointed to be last, but pleased that he had at least made the journey safely. From that day, the cycle of years was named in the order the animals completed their race; it is said that you will share some of the characteristics of the animal in whose year you were born.

REFLECTION

Discuss with the children the fact that characteristics we attribute to certain creatures are quite different from those attributed to the same creatures in other cultures. So it is a good illustration of the fact that we must never jump to conclusions. Point out to pupils that in many cultures it is not considered polite to ask the ages of adults, so it can be very useful instead for people to just say which of the twelve animal years they were born in. This is of course an excellent indicator of age!

Prayer

Dear God,
Thank you for giving us the chance to hear and enjoy many stories from around the world. Help us to understand the lessons that can be learned from appreciating the tales and traditions that are important to other people.
Amen

Song

Sing Hosanna   (Alleluya, 3: *A&C Black*)

Chinese New Year 2

Do you have any of the traits of the creature who shares the name of the year in which you were born?

1996	Rat	Works hard at night but enjoys an easier life during the day.
1997	Ox	Strong and faithful, enjoys a happy and successful life.
1998	Tiger	Intelligent – this person will do well in life.
1999	Hare	Happy and successful, this person will have many children.
2000	Dragon	Likes an easy life, angers quickly if children are endangered.
2001	Snake	Quick, wise and able to tackle many jobs.
2002	Horse	Strong and friendly; enjoys doing good.
2003	Ram	A good leader; proud and enjoys helping others.
2004	Monkey	Nimble, curious and often rather noisy.
2005	Cockerel	A proud and industrious early riser.
2006	Dog	A good friend, quick to learn new things.
2007	Pig	Intelligent and a good parent; angers easily.

Moses in the bulrushes

This story would be ideal to use at around the time of Mothering Sunday.

 AIM: To raise children's awareness of a story from the Old Testament that shows the love of a mother for her child.

PREPARATION

■ Prior to the assembly, photocopy the sihouettes from page 33 on to paper so that they can be cut out and used on the OHP at appropriate points in the story.

INTRODUCTION

Today's assembly story comes from the Old Testament of the Bible. The Old Testament contains stories that took place long before Jesus was born. The story is about the Israelites at the time when they lived in Egypt and the king of Egypt made them into slaves. I have two questions for you before we start the story: Do you know the special name for a king of Egypt? Do you know what slaves are? Invite and discuss answers to the questions.

STORY

The poor Israelite slaves had to work very hard for the Pharaoh's people. The people in charge were called slave-drivers and they would whip the slaves if they stopped to take a rest. Pharaoh was worried that the slaves might fight back and turn against him. He decided that there were too many Israelites and that he needed to reduce their numbers. He ordered his people to search the houses of the Israelite people to find every baby boy, then to take these babies to the River Nile and drown them. (Put the silhouette of the Nile on the OHP.)

The news quickly spread from house to house in the Israelite towns. People tried to hide their baby boys but it was very difficult because babies often make a lot of noise so the soldiers quickly found them and carried them off to the river. There were many sad families.

One family who had two children, a girl called Miriam and a boy called Aaron. Aaron was safe because he wasn't a baby, but then the mother, whose name was Jochebed, gave birth to a baby boy. Everybody in the family was very worried because they loved the new baby so much. They managed to hide him for a few weeks but they realised that it was getting more and more difficult. Then Jochebed had an idea. Jochebed knew that the Pharaoh's daughter bathed in the river every day. The princess would always come to the same spot with her servants, not far from where Jochebed and her family lived. If only the princess could find a baby there, surely she would not want it to be killed.

Jochebed gathered some wide flat reeds from the river and carefully wove them into the shape of a basket. She coated the outside of the basket with tar and lined the inside with a soft, warm blanket. Then she kissed her baby and placed him in the basket and, when no-one was looking, hurried down to the river. She placed the basket in the reeds where the river wouldn't float it away. (Place the basket in amongst the reeds.)

Miriam stayed to keep watch. She waited and waited until eventually the princess came to bathe in the river as usual. The princess suddenly spotted the basket and, wondering what it was, asked her servant to fetch it. There inside, of course, was the beautiful baby boy and, just as Jochebed had hoped, the princess decided that she would adopt the baby herself. Miriam rushed over to her. "I know a lady who could nurse the baby for you," she said.

REFLECTION

Who do you think that lady was? Does anybody know what name was given to the baby?

Prayer

Dear God,
Thank you for the love of our mothers, for the care they give us and for the ways in which they look after us. Help us to show them that we love them too.   *Amen*

Song

Moses, I know you're the man   (Alleluya, 73: *A&C Black*)

Moses grows up

 AIM: To continue the story of Moses.

PREPARATION

■ Photocopy and cut out the silhouettes from page 35 for use on the OHP. If possible, show the children some real bulrushes before starting the story.

INTRODUCTION

Do you remember the story of Moses being found in the reeds by the Egyptian princess? We often hear about 'Moses in the bulrushes'. Bulrushes are tall reeds with long velvety heads that contain the seeds of the plant. Do you remember which part of the Bible the story comes from? The Israelites were living in Egypt and they were slaves. The Egyptian king, the Pharaoh, thought there were too many Israelites so he decided to stop their numbers growing. Moses' mother rescued him by getting the Pharaoh's daughter to bring him up. In today's story we are going to find out what happened to Moses after that.

STORY

Moses was a very lucky boy. He lived in a beautiful palace and he was looked after by the Egyptian princess. He learned many things but the most important thing that he learned was that the Egyptian slave-drivers were very cruel to his people, the Israelites. One day, when he was grown up, he saw an Egyptian kill one of the Israelites; he rushed over and hit the Egyptian so hard that he killed him. He hid the body in the sand.

Moses realised that he had done wrong and he also realised that he would be in terrible trouble when the king found out so he ran away to the desert to a land called Midian. He lived there for many years; he even met a young woman there, called Zipporah, and he married her. He worked for Zipporah's father, taking care of the sheep and goats. This was a big change in his life: he had lived as a prince in Egypt and now he was living as a shepherd. (Place silhouette of Moses on OHP.)

One day Moses was leading his flock of sheep and goats across the desert when he saw a bush burning. (Add the burning bush to the OHP.) *It was very strange because, although there were flames coming from the bush, the leaves and branches were not actually burning at all. Then a voice called to Moses from the centre of the bush:*
"Moses! Do not come any closer. Take off your sandals because you are on holy ground. I am the God of your ancestors." Moses covered his face with his hands because he was afraid to look at God. God spoke again.
"I have seen that my people are suffering in Egypt. You are to go to the king of Egypt so that you can lead my people out of the country."

Moses was very worried. He thought that the king would not listen to him but he also thought that the Israelites would not follow him. God spoke again: "Throw your stick on to the ground." Moses threw his stick down and, as it touched the ground, it turned into a snake (Add picture of snake on to the OHP.); *he was terrified. "Pick up the snake by the tail." Moses bent down and picked up the snake, which immediately turned back into his stick. "Do this to prove to the Israelites that the Lord has appeared before you."*

REFLECTION

Are you ever afraid to do the right thing? Moses was afraid to go back to Egypt even though it was the right thing to do.

Prayer

Dear God,
Please help us always to do the right thing, even when the right thing is very difficult.
Help us to be brave and honest and caring towards other people. *Amen*

Song

Moses, I know you're the man (Alleluya, 73: *A&C Black*)

Moses grows up

Moses leads his people from Egypt

 AIM: To continue the story of Moses

PREPARATION

■ Photocopy the illustration on page 37 on to an OHP transparency.

INTRODUCTION

Remind the pupils of the story of Moses so far:

You remember that God asked Moses to lead the Israelites out of Egypt; today we will hear what happened next.

STORY

God arranged for Moses to meet his brother and sister again. Do you remember their names? Aaron went with Moses to see the Pharaoh, but as God had told Moses, Pharaoh did not want to let the people go. So God sent punishments to the Egyptians: he made the water of the River Nile turn red, he created a plague of frogs, he created plagues of flies, the cattle began to die, there was a hailstorm with huge hailstones and there was a plague of locusts. Do you know what locusts are? They fly in swarms and if they land on a bush or a tree they eat every single leaf. But with every plague, the king of Egypt still refused to let the Israelites go. (Place illustration on OHP.)

The most awful thing was when the eldest son of every family in Egypt died. But the sons of the Israelite families did not die – the plague of death passed over them. Even now, Jewish people still celebrate this with a special feast called the feast of the Passover.

At last, the Pharaoh decided to let Moses and his people go – he could stand the punishments no longer. Quickly the Israelites prepared to leave, then they set off on their journey. They had nearly left Egypt when Pharaoh changed his mind and sent his army to chase them but when the Israelites reached the sea the waters parted to let them through then closed in again, stopping the Pharaoh's army from following.

The Israelites were free. But now they had to go and live in the desert where there was no food so God sent food every night for the people to find when they woke up in the morning. This special food was called manna.

Moses continued to lead the people, taking them to a mountain called Mount Sinai. This was a very special place because here God gave his people his special laws to follow. The laws were called the ten commandments.

REFLECTION

Let's think about some of the laws that God gave. These are still very important today. Do not kill another human being. Do not steal. Do not tell lies. Do not be greedy.

Prayer

Dear God,
Help us to be good. Help us not to hurt other people. Help us not to steal or to tell lies or to be greedy. *Amen*

Song

Moses, I know you're the man   (Alleluya, 73: *A&C Black*)

Moses leads his people from Egypt

Spring

 AIM: Celebrating new life in spring and appreciating the way different faiths celebrate festivals at this time of year.

PREPARATION

■ Photocopy the information on page 39 on to an OHP transparency or you may prefer to make an enlarged version on bigger paper for a wall display.

INTRODUCTION

We have just about left winter weather behind us now and reached spring time.
What do you think of when the word spring is mentioned? Accept responses – you may wish to write these on to OHP acetate, whiteboard or flip chart so that they are seen as valued answers and a reminder throughout the assembly. At this stage the responses are likely to be about weather, flowers or blossom.

ACTIVITY

Can you tell me any of the religious festivals or celebrations that also occur in the spring?

Accept responses – these are likely to include any or all of the festivals on the background information sheet accompanying this assembly. The sheet is also suitable for wall display. If you do display the sheet, explain to the pupils that not all religions are shown – perhaps they know some more festivals or could research these. Add answers to those you have already written.

Would anyone like to tell us a little about any of these festivals?

Consider each of the festivals with the pupils one at a time – using the background sheet if needed to help with basic information.

Whilst the festivals we have considered all take place in the spring, do you think any of them have particular links with the spring season?

Accept responses; hopefully these will include the fact that Holi has an evident link to the changing seasons.

REFLECTION

It is important that we enjoy, and think about the religious festivals that we take part in with our families, and that we respect the beliefs of others as they enjoy their celebrations.

Prayer

Dear God,
Help us to participate thoughtfully in the festivals that we celebrate with others who share our faith. Help us also to enjoy the beauty of the earth as the season changes from winter to spring. Thank you for the new life we see all around us as the earth warms up, seeds grow, and new life is created.
Amen

Song

Morning has broken   (Someone's Singing, Lord 3: *A&C Black*)
or
English Country Garden   (Harlequin, 22: *A&C Black*)

Spring

Religious festivals occurring in the spring

Easter

The Christian festival of Easter celebrates the resurrection of Jesus the Sunday after his crucifixion on the day known as Good Friday. Christians believe that Jesus was the son of God and his earthly existence was needed to save people from their sins. The Easter festival happens in March or April.

Passover (Pesakh)

This is a Jewish festival that celebrates the escape of the Israelites from their slavery in Egypt. Its title is a reminder of the night when the angel of death 'passed over' the specially marked Jewish homes without harming their children.

Baisakhi

In April each year this Sikh festival celebrates the founding of the Khalsa. The khalsa represents a willingness to defend the Sikh faith and to care for the poor or needy from any religion.

Holi

The Hindu festival of Holi is an enjoyable celebration that usually takes place over two days. On the first evening public bonfires are lit. The following day people spray their family and friends with coloured water and powders. This festival is commonly known as the festival of colours and is a time when winter is cast off and everyone enjoys the colours and new life of the spring. There are also a number of Hindu legends that are commemorated by the Holi celebrations.

The swallows return

Ideally this assembly should take place at the very end of March or early in April.

 AIM: To encourage feelings of awe and wonder in relation to nature, specifically the migratory journeys of the swallows.

PREPARATION

- Photocopy and cut out the silhouette of a swallow from page 41.
- Photocopy the world map from page 42 on to an OHP transparency

---

■ INTRODUCTION

In our last assembly we talked about signs of spring. In the summer term we will be talking about some special expressions or sayings called proverbs. I have a proverb for you today: one swallow doesn't make a summer. What do you think that means? Before you answer that question, here's another question: what is a swallow? Obtain responses. *I'll show you a picture of a swallow.* (Place the silhouette of the swallow on to the OHP.)

One swallow doesn't make a summer. What does that mean? Obtain responses.

■ ACTIVITY

Now is the time of year to keep a look out for swallows because they are just arriving in our country having made an incredibly perilous and difficult journey. Some of you may have been on holiday to Spain or even to Africa. (Place the map on to the OHP so that you can point out Spain and Africa.) *Spain is a country in southern Europe and Africa is a whole continent made of lots of countries. If you have been on holiday to Spain or Africa you will know what a long way it is to travel. If we visit Africa we have to travel by aeroplane and it takes a few hours to travel there because it is thousands of kilometres away. The amazing thing is that that is where the swallows are travelling from. They can't travel in an aeroplane, they have to fly using their own wings. Every year they fly to our country from Africa so that they can build their nests here, lay their eggs and raise their young. Then, in the autumn, they fly all the way back to Africa.*

■ REFLECTION

When we see the first swallow in spring we can get quite excited for two reasons: one reason is because we know that the swallow has travelled thousands of kilometres to be here and the other is because we know summer is on its way. One swallow doesn't make a summer but it does show that summer is coming.

Prayer

Dear God,
Thank you for nature all around us. Thank you for the spring time and the arrival of the first swallow that shows that summer is coming soon. Amen

Song

Morning has broken (Someone's Singing, Lord 3: *A&C Black*)

The swallows return 2

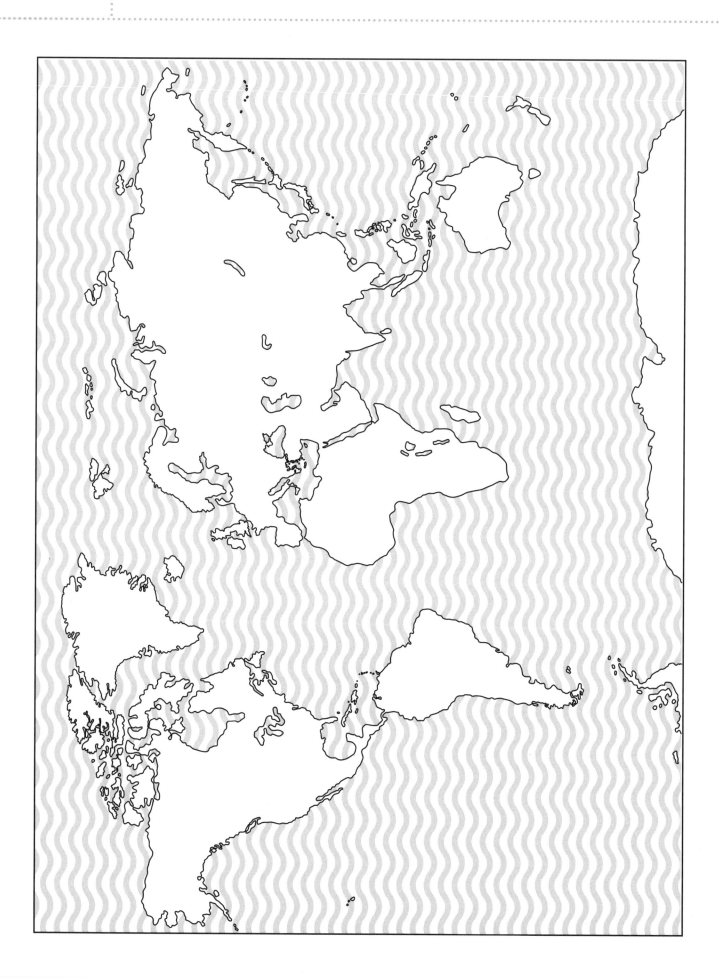

Let's talk

 AIM: To encourage children to be aware of others in the school.

PREPARATION

- This assembly is similar to the assembly 'Mingle, mingle' in Assembly Today for Key Stage 1 but it extends the activity to include the use of questions. You may like to present this assembly with only part of the school present as there will be some movement around the hall.
- This assembly is very effective in encouraging children to talk politely to others. We suggest that pupils in Year 6 should meet those in Year 4 and pupils in Year 5 should meet those in Year 3 but you may like to arrange the assembly differently.
- As always, we present a 'script' for you to follow if you wish to, but you can present the assembly in any way that suits you.

INTRODUCTION

What do you think teachers say to you most often? Obtain responses – these could be interesting!
I know some things that teachers used to say a lot when I was at school: 'Don't talk!' 'Be quiet!' 'Stop talking!' Of course, it is important to stop talking sometimes. When should we not be talking? Obtain responses – hopefully the children will give answers such as 'when we should be working' or 'when someone else is speaking'.

Today I'm going to ask you to talk to somebody else but not your friend or even anybody else in your class. Don't start talking yet. I am going to ask you to get up from your place and go to meet someone in the class that is two years below yours or two years above yours so if you are in Year 4 you will meet someone in Year 6 and if you are in Year 3 you will meet someone in Year 5. When you meet them, what could you talk about? You could tell them your name; you could say how old you are; you could ask them some questions. What questions could you ask? You could ask them when their birthday is; you could ask them where they live; you could ask them what their favourite subject is at school.

ACTIVITY

Are you ready? Don't talk yet. I will give you some time for a short conversation but when I clap my hands I would like you to stop and look at me. Now, stand up and go to meet someone from another class.

Allow time for the children to move and hold a short conversation then clap your hands.

Now I am going to ask you to move away from the person you have been talking to and find somebody else: if you have been talking to a boy find a girl to speak to and if you have been talking to a girl find a boy to speak to. Are you ready? Go.

After a short conversation, clap your hands again and ask the children to sit facing the front where they are. When you end the assembly the children should still be able to leave class by class.

REFLECTION

Today you were asked to talk and you should have met someone new. You should have been able to ask that person some questions politely and you should have had polite replies. Remember that everybody here is part of our school community and everybody should be polite to each other and caring towards each other.

Prayer

Dear God,
Please help us to play our part as a member of our school community.
Please help us to be polite and caring towards everybody in our school.   Amen

♫
Song   Look out for loneliness   (Someone's Singing, Lord 36: *A&C Black*)

Turning over a new leaf

Ideally this assembly should be the first in the Summer Term.

 AIM: To encourage some children to consider a fresh start.

> **PREPARATION**
> ■ Do not tell the children the title of the assembly.
> ■ Pick a leaf from a tree, if there are any freshly grown leaves yet. If not, photocopy and cut out the silhouette of the leaf from page 45. Place the leaf or the silhouette on the OHP but cover it with a sheet of card so that it is not visible to the pupils until you are ready.

INTRODUCTION

Do you know that at the start of every new year lots of people make New Year Resolutions? We make New Year Resolutions when we decide that we want to do something differently for the whole year. Perhaps we have done something wrong in the past and we want to make a fresh start. The start of a new term is a bit like the start of a new year.

ACTIVITY

I am going to show you something and I am going to do something with it. You will realise what the thing is as soon as you see it and you should be able to see what I am doing with it. What I am looking for is somebody who can tell me the famous expression that I am demonstrating. You will need to watch very carefully. You will need to concentrate so don't talk about it. Only when you think that you know what this famous expression is should you put your hand up. I will ask someone to tell me, when I am ready to. Please don't call out and don't talk. Are you ready?

Reveal the leaf then turn it over in an exaggerated fashion! You may wish to demonstrate this several times, reminding pupils not to call out or talk. Hopefully someone will correctly identify your action as 'turning over a new leaf'.

I think that turning over a new leaf really means turning over a new page of a book because we sometimes call the pages of a book its leaves. If we turn over a new page we can have a blank page to start on. We have a clean piece of paper to make a fresh start.

REFLECTION

So what does the expression 'turning over a new leaf' mean? It can mean deciding not to do bad things any more. It can mean working harder. It can mean helping more at home. Have a good think: do you need to turn over a new leaf? It's a new term, we can make a new start.

Prayer

Dear God,
Help each of us to decide whether we need to turn over a new leaf. Do we need a fresh start? Can we have a fresh start? Help us this term to be good to each other and to work hard at school. Help us to be good at home too. Perhaps we can help more and make our families' lives a little easier.
                                                                    Amen

Song

It's me, O Lord   (Alleluya, 51: *A&C Black*)

Proverbs

 AIM: To encourage children to find the meanings of proverbs and to consider how they may affect our behaviour.

PREPARATION

■ Photocopy the proverbs sheet from page 47 on to an OHP transparency to be shown during the assembly.

▨ INTRODUCTION

Do you remember the famous expression that we talked about in the last assembly?

You may need to remind the pupils by demonstrating the turning over of a new leaf.

▨ ACTIVITY

Show the OHP transparency that lists the proverbs but cover the title while you ask the pupils:

Does anybody know the special name for these sayings?

The special sayings are called proverbs

Reveal the title at the top of the page.

Let's have a look at some of them:

Many hands make light work – what do you think that means?

Too many cooks spoil the broth – what does that mean? Does anybody know what broth is?

Those two proverbs are both good sayings. 'Many hands make light work' means that if lots of people help a job is easier to do – that's true isn't it? But 'too many cooks spoil the broth' means that if too many people help the job can get ruined because people get in the way – that's true as well. So although the two proverbs seem to be opposite to each other they are both true.

Let's look at some more:

The early bird catches the worm – what do you think that means?

Make hay while the sun shines – what does that mean?

In some ways those two proverbs are not opposites but nearly the same. They both mean that people who get on with a job will achieve more.

You may wish to discuss the other proverbs on the transparency or simply to leave them on the screen for pupils to think about.

▨ REFLECTION

Let's think about the proverbs in relation to our lives. Do we 'make hay while the sun shines'? Do we help each other because 'many hands make light work'?

Over the next few days, see if you hear any proverbs in use. Somebody in your family might say a proverb or somebody on the television might say a proverb. You may be surprised how often these very old sayings are actually used.

Prayer

Dear God,
Please help us to get our work done properly – help us to 'make hay while the sun shines'. Remind us to help other people because 'many hands make light work' but don't let us get in the way because 'too many cooks spoil the broth'. Amen

Song

With a little help from my friends   (Alleluya, 38: *A&C Black*)

 Andrew Brodie: Assembly Today KS2 © A&C Black Publishers Ltd. 2005

Proverbs

Many hands make light work.

Too many cooks spoil the broth.

The early bird catches the worm.

Make hay while the sun shines.

Don't count your chickens before they are hatched.

You can lead a horse to water but you can't make it drink.

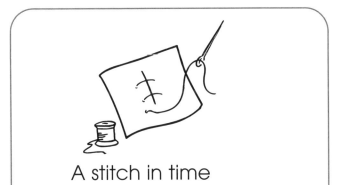

A stitch in time saves nine.

Look before you leap.

Opposites

AIM: To encourage pupils to value each other even where they are completely different from each other.

PREPARATION

- Photocopy the words on page 49 on to an OHP transparency to be displayed during the assembly. Have five coloured whiteboard pens available.
- During the course of the assembly you will invite pupils out to draw lines joining the opposites.
- You may also like to have two magnets available.
- We have shown the assembly as a script but you will, of course, wish to present it in your own words.

■ INTRODUCTION

Do you remember the assembly where we looked at very old sayings? Do you remember what those sayings are called? Two of the proverbs seemed to be opposite to each other and yet, when we thought about them, we found that they were both true in their own way. Do you remember what those two proverbs were?

■ ACTIVITY

Today we are looking at some more opposites. I am going to show them on the screen. See if you can match the words on the left with the words on the right. Please don't talk about it yet – you will have a chance to talk in a minute. For now, just look carefully at the two lists of words and see if you can match them up.

Would someone like to come out and help me?

Choose five (A, B, C, D, E) people to come out; issue each of them with a coloured pen.

Now, you are going to tell my helpers which words to join together. Let's look at the first word on the left: big. What's the opposite of big?

Correct, small is the opposite of big so would A please join 'big' to 'small'.

What's the opposite of tall?

Correct, short is the opposite of big so would B please join 'short' to 'big'.

Continue so that all the pairs of opposites are matched up.

■ REFLECTION

I would like you to think very carefully about these opposites. Now think about your best friend. Are you exactly the same as your best friend? There will be some things about you that are the same and there will be some things about you that are quite different. In fact, you may be opposites in some ways. There's an old saying, not a proverb but a saying, that 'opposites attract' – it means that sometimes people who are really different match up well. We also say 'opposites attract' when we look at magnets because the north pole of a magnet is attracted to the south pole of another magnet.

Prayer

Dear God,
Please help us to respect other people even if they are quite different to us: tall or short, blue-eyed or brown-eyed, boy or girl, black or white, people who love sport or don't love sport, people who are good at maths or people who find maths hard.   Amen

Song

The ink is black, the page is white   (Someone's Singing, Lord 39: *A&C Black*)

---

big	heavy
tall	white
left	dark
black	small
hot	dry
light	day
light	short
night	right
soft	cold
wet	hard

New at school 1

AIM: To encourage a willingness to understand and support others.

PREPARATION

■ Photocopy the passage of writing from page 51 on to OHP transparency.

■ **INTRODUCTION**

We all like to think we are fair and that we don't make hasty judgements about people, but I wonder whether we really are as good to other people as we like to believe.

I am going to tell you today about a new boy at a school and how he was treated by his classmates. What you are about to hear is based on a true story – so although it may sound like fiction there is a lot in it that you might recognise. There may even be parts that make you feel a little uncomfortable!

Slowly and carefully read the passage on the following page – you may show the text on the OHP after you have read it if you wish to have it as a focus for the ensuing discussion.

Ask the pupils what they have learned about the new boy. Answers should include that he came from abroad so he couldn't speak English. He looked different and probably was quite poor. He found it difficult to communicate at first without language.

Ask what they think of the sentiments in the last verse. We may all be guilty of excusing ourselves for giving up trying to help another and using the excuse that he/she should do more.

Ask whether they think the new boy's first few weeks at school were happy ones, and why / why not. Hopefully at this point it will be realised that the other children though not perhaps overtly cruel may have added to his sense of isolation.

Finally ask why they think each verse ends with 'But they didn't know the truth'. If there is time to spare you may wish to ask pupils what they think 'the truth' might be.

Explain that in the next assembly you will be reading another passage that will explain the life of the new boy at school from his point of view.

■ **REFLECTION**

It is not always easy to support other people that are finding life difficult. When people are a little different from us and don't easily fit in with our ways of life, it is often the case that those people have their lives made even more difficult by our attitudes. It is important to always try our very best to help them to feel at ease and to try to learn more about what they like to do and what would make them happy.

Prayer

Dear Lord,
Help us to use our hearts and minds to welcome strangers into our community. Give us the wisdom not to judge others on their clothing, language or appearance.   *Amen*

♫

Song

When I needed a neighbour   (Someone's Singing, Lord 35: *A&C Black*)

New at school 1

He arrived at school looking pale.
He didn't seem to want to speak.
They started to think he was rather strange.
Their teacher explained that he had come from abroad.
But they didn't know the truth.

His haircut was not the best.
He had no sense of style.
His clothes were faded and ill fitting.
He kept himself to himself.
But they didn't know the truth.

He started to speak to the others.
His words were faltering, his accent heavy.
He didn't always manage to find the correct words,
Though he tried his very best.
But they didn't know the truth.

He watched them in the playground.
They talked about how strange he was.
He struggled to write in English.
They didn't choose to sit by him.
But they didn't know the truth.

His language improved and he worked hard.
But he was still different from them.
He didn't know the best football teams,
And wasn't interested in the same things as them.
But they didn't know the truth.

They thought they were being fair.
After all he should make some effort too.
Why should they always be the ones
To try to help him to feel part of things?
But of course ...they didn't know the truth!

New at school 2

 AIM: To see things from the perspectives of others.

PREPARATION

■ Photocopy the passage of writing from page 53 on to OHP transparency.

▓ INTRODUCTION

In our last assembly we looked at how easy it is for us to make life less comfortable for newcomers than it needs to be. We heard about a new boy at a school. It was obvious that for many reasons he would find it hard to settle in – but we didn't learn much that would make us believe that the other children really did their very best to help him. They forgot that it was not only on the first day that the new boy needed support, especially as he had to learn to speak our language and fit in with our ways of life.

Today we are going to find out more about the new boy himself.

Read the passage from the next page – you may then wish to put it on the OHP to be a focus for the ensuing discussion.

Ask the pupils what we have now found out that we didn't know before.

Discuss with them, how we now know what might have made it much harder for the new boy to settle.

This is also an appropriate point, if time allows, to discuss the word 'prejudice' and how it results from our not understanding other people and often feeling threatened by them: prejudice is born of ignorance and fear.

▓ REFLECTION

The new boy had obviously had a very difficult time, and at his new school the reactions of others did not help him much. It is important that we do not judge others on appearances, and that we make every effort to welcome others into out communities.

Prayer

Dear God,
Help us to remember that we are all part of one family – the human race. Help us to remember that you know and love us all for our unique identities. We thank you for the opportunity to meet different kinds of people and to learn to understand them better. Amen

♫
Song

God Knows Me   (Come and Praise, 15: *BBC Books*)

New at school 2

I arrived at the school feeling tired and confused.
I didn't understand what they were saying.
They talked to me loudly, but I didn't know their words.
I wanted to cry, but I didn't.
Why did our lives have to change?

Things hadn't been the same since dad
had been taken away.
Mum sobbed, I didn't know how to help.
We were alone and in danger.
We had to escape the home I had always known.
Why did our lives have to change?

We arrived on a lorry.
It had been our dark smelly home for days.
We had nothing except the clothes we wore.
There had been no time to pack.
Why did our lives have to change?

We were now safe but I didn't like it.
I had to wear cast off clothes.
The others looked at me suspiciously
I felt alone and empty.
Why did our lives have to change?

As I learned my new language, life eased a bit.
Still I didn't know their ways and their games.
I didn't feel like one of them yet,
However hard I tried.
Why did our lives have to change?

Is my father still alive? I may never know.
Will my mother ever laugh again? I hope so.
Will I ever feel I belong here? Who knows?
Perhaps one day I will be accepted here.
I had no choice, my life had to change.

Andrew Brodie: Assembly Today KS2 © A&C Black Publishers Ltd. 2005

Silver

 AIM: Appreciation of and responses to the beauty of the world at night time.

PREPARATION

■ Photocopy the poem from page 55 on to OHP transparency.

▨ INTRODUCTION

What colours do you associate with outdoors in the night time?

Accept and discuss responses.

Often people only think about the darkness of night, but in fact there is a lot of silvery beauty associated with it too.

Can you think of things that might appear silver at night?

Accept and discuss responses as appropriate.

▨ MAIN ACTIVITY

We are going to look at a very well known poem by a famous poet called Walter De La Mare. He had looked at the silvery quality of the night and describes it in his poem called 'Silver'.

Put the poem 'Silver' on the OHP and read it to the pupils.

After reading the poem, ask the pupils what they think causes everything to appear silver in the poem. (Hopefully the children will have realised that it is the moon that causes this).

Reread the poem asking pupils to keep a mental count of how many things appear silver by the light of the moon. After the second reading ask pupils to name the silver things in the poem. Point out that most of the silver things belong to the natural world eg the dog's paws, fruit on the trees, fish and parts of the mouse.

▨ REFLECTION

Prayer

Dear God,
We thank you for the many beautiful things to be seen at night. We thank you particularly for the silvery moon, the beauty it brings to the earth, and the light it reflects on to the world during the hours of darkness.   *Amen*

Song

I watch the Sunrise   (Alleluya, 15: *A&C Black*)
or
Silver Trumpet   (Alleluya, 26: *A&C Black*)

          Andrew Brodie: Assembly Today KS2 © A&C Black Publishers Ltd. 2005

Silver

Silver

Slowly, silently now the moon

Walks the night in her silver shoon;

This way and that, she peers, and sees

Silver fruit upon silver trees;

One by one the casements catch

Her beams beneath the silvery thatch;

Couched in his kennel, like a log,

With paws of silver sleeps the dog;

From their shadowy cote the white breasts peep

Of doves in a silver feathered sleep;

A harvest mouse goes scampering by,

With silver claws, and silver eye;

And moveless fish in the water gleam,

By silver reeds in a silver stream.

Walter de la Mare

Is your cup half empty or half full?

 AIM: To encourage self awareness.

PREPARATION

■ Photocopy the diary extracts from pages 57 and 58 on to OHP transparencies.

▨ INTRODUCTION

At the beginning of this assembly ask the children what they think it means when we speak of some people living life as if their cup is 'half full' whilst for other people their cups always seem to be half empty. Accept their answers and ensure they understand that the 'saying' refers to more positive or more negative views of the same situation.

▨ MAIN FOCUS

Explain that the pupils will be shown two diary extracts. They are from the diaries of cousins that went on a family holiday together. The children, who were about the same age, stayed on a campsite near the beach. The extracts will be seen and considered separately, and pupils should consider what they learn about the characters of the writers. Point out to the pupils that both the children had an enjoyable holiday! Show the first extract on the OHP – read it aloud to the pupils and ask them if they wish to make any comments about it.

Next reveal the second extract – remind the pupils that it refers to exactly the same holiday – and read it through in the same way as the previous one.

▨ REFLECTION

The enjoyment we get out of life can depend very much on our own attitudes. The person who believes that everything goes wrong for them tends to notice and dwell on life's misfortunes whilst the person that looks on the brighter side of life despite the misfortunes that can occur from time to time seems to have a happier more contented life.

Ask the children to spend a minute quietly thinking about themselves and whether they feel they usually manage to focus on the positive aspects of their lives.

Prayer

Dear God,
Please help us to appreciate the good things that happen in our lives, and give us the strength that we need to cope positively with less fortunate events.　　　*Amen*

Song

Happiness is   (Alleluya, 5: *A&C Black*)
or
I like the Flowers   (Flying A Round, 43: *A&C Black*)

Is your cup half empty or half full? 1

Diary A

Today was the first proper day of our holiday.

Got up this morning and felt very excited to see the sun shining. After breakfast we headed for the beach. The sand was soft and near the water's edge it was just right for making sandcastles. Lunch was a picnic – it's strange how much tastier sandwiches seem when you are having a good day out. An hour after we had eaten, the adults said we could swim in the sea if we were careful. It was great jumping through waves and splashing about in the water.

At about 5 o'clock we went back to the campsite. It was a warm evening so we had a barbeque to round off the day.

Fell into bed, very tired, at 9 o'clock. Have written my diary and I am ready to fall asleep!

I wonder what we'll be doing tomorrow?

Is your cup half empty or half full? 2

Diary B

This is the first day of our holiday, sleeping in a tent was O.K. though I think it would have been better to stay in a hotel.

noisy →

The weather was good so we went to the beach. I was surprised how dark the sand was – I thought it should have been a golden colour. We made sandcastles – I thought it was rather a childish thing to be doing but the adults seemed to think it was 'the thing to do' when you went to the beach.

There was a picnic at lunch time. It tasted good but somehow eating on the beach always means you end up with sand in your sandwiches!

crunch crunch

It was really boring after lunch as we had to wait a whole hour 'for our food to go down' before we were allowed to go in the sea. When we got back to the campsite we had a barbeque as the weather was still warm. Now we are in bed and it's only 9 o'clock (I think it's unfair having to come to bed so early when we are on holiday) perhaps we'll be allowed to stay up later tomorrow.

Andrew Brodie: Assembly Today KS2 © A&C Black Publishers Ltd. 2005

The chess board

AIM: To encourage pupils to consider the effects of kindness and unkindness.

PREPARATION
- Photocopy the chess board on page 60 on to OHP transparency.
- Prepare some small beads to represent grains of wheat.

INTRODUCTION
I wonder if you have ever heard the story of the man who asked to be paid for his work by being given grains of wheat. This story was first told about eight hundred years ago by an Arab mathematician called Ibn Kallikan.

ACTIVITY
Place the picture of the chess board on the OHP.

Do you know how many squares there are on the chess board? There are eight rows of eight squares so that's sixty-four altogether because eight eights are sixty-four. The man asked to be paid for sixty-four days. He wanted just one grain of wheat for his first day's work, then two for the second day then four for the third day.

Place the single grain, or bead, on to the first square of the board, then two grains on the second square and four grains on the third square.

Can you see what's happening? The amount he gets paid doubles every day. So how much would he be paid on the fourth day? Place eight grains on the fourth square.

Now I'm not going to put on any more grains just yet. I'm going to ask some of the older children to try to work out, in their heads, how much the man would be paid on the eighth day, that's the last square on the top line on the board.

Wait for responses – the answer should be 128. What about the ninth square? Continue until you feel that the pupils are beginning to realise just how quickly the quantities are now growing through the doubling process.

Do you see how rich the man is becoming? Imagine they were pound coins instead of grains of wheat – if I was paid in this way I would become very rich very quickly. Perhaps some of you could work out how much I would be paid on the sixty-fourth square – you could work this out in your spare time.

REFLECTION
Instead of grains of wheat or pound coins, let's consider acts of kindness. If I am kind to someone, they are likely to be kind back to me and because this makes both of us in a happy mood we are likely to be kind to two other people. Now there are four happy people so we are kind to four other people and now there are eight happy people – the kindness grows and grows.

Prayer

Dear God,
Please help us to spread kindness and happiness. Help us to remember that kindness grows and grows and we can play our part in helping it to grow.　　　　*Amen*

Song　Magic Penny　(Alleluya, 10: *A&C Black*)

The chess board

Tangrams

AIM: To encourage children to observe how separate parts of a unit can work well together and, in particular, to value the school as a community.

PREPARATION

- This activity works particularly well in a seven class school but, in other situations, you can classify your school into seven units. For example: the teachers, the cleaners, the school office plus four classes; or Reception plus Years 1 to 6.
- Photocopy page 62 on to card, then cut out the tangram pieces as shown. Photocopy page 62 again on to an OHP transparency so that your card pieces can be placed on the transparency during the assembly.

INTRODUCTION

Place the transparency on to the OHP.

Have a good look at the square on this sheet. Can you see how many pieces it has been divided into? I have copied the square and cut it out. Look.

Place the seven pieces in position on the square.

Now look at the other pictures on the screen. The picture of the sailing boat can be made exactly out of the seven pieces of my square. Let's see if anybody can make the sailing boat picture using my seven pieces – have we got any volunteers?

Invite a child out to try piecing the shapes together correctly on to the outline of the boat. Repeat this for the pictures of the dog and the wrapped sweet.

REFLECTION

These pictures are called tangram puzzles. Tangram puzzles are made of seven pieces. They remind me of our school: our school has seven pieces and just like the tangrams all the pieces work together. The pieces are different from each other and sometimes they seem to go off in different directions but they still all fit together. Just like the tangrams they seem to make different shapes but the pieces of the school always come back together to make a whole community. Assembly time is the best time to see our school community together, just like the tangram square.

Prayer

Dear God,
Thank you for our school community. The school is made of different pieces; please help those pieces to fit together well. Help us to look after our school community; help us to care for everyone in our school. Amen

Song   When I needed a neighbour   (Someone's Singing, Lord 35: *A&C Black*)

Tangrams

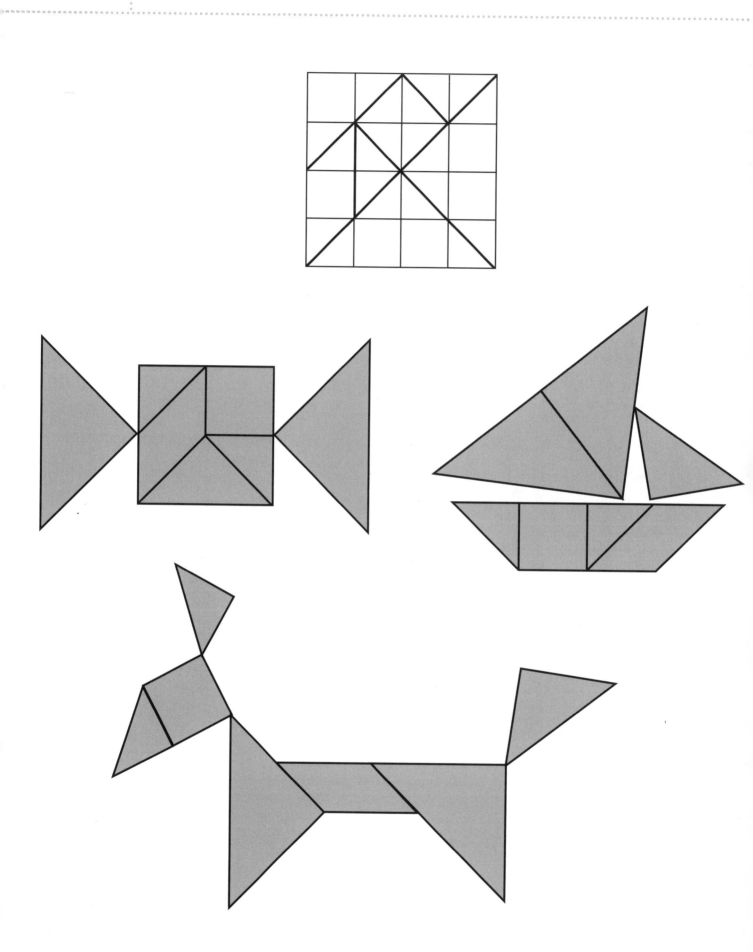

Andrew Brodie: Assembly Today KS2 © A&C Black Publishers Ltd. 2005

Common values

AIM: To encourage pupils to consider what they believe is right, and to use this knowledge to reflect on their own way of living.

PREPARATION
■ Photocopy the information from page 64 on to an OHP transparency.

INTRODUCTION

Many people living in the same community belong to different religions, or even say they do not follow any particular faith. You would think this might make us all have very different values, but in this assembly we will look at what we each believe and see if people are really as different as we might have thought.

MAIN ACTIVITY

I would like you to all think about what is important to you. Your beliefs will reflect your religious, cultural and family life. They will also be things that you have thought about during your life and have come to value for a great many reasons.

At this point you should arrange with the pupils how they will indicate their response. For example they might use a thumbs up for agreement and thumbs down for disagreement – or a simple show of hands. You may find it appropriate to indicate that partaking in this is optional as not all children may wish to share their beliefs.

1 It is important to be truthful.
2 Family life is important.
3 Other people should not be harmed.
4 There is a God.
5 It is important to care for the environment.
6 You should help people in need

REFLECTION

It is interesting that we are all such different people with different lives, and yet in many important ways we have the same ideas and values.
Now I will show you a sheet of some important aspects of the beliefs and values of some of the major religious groups.
As you can see, though there can be some great variations of beliefs and customs, many major values are the same in most or all faiths. When you see this it makes you realise that it should be quite easy for people of different faiths to live side by side peacefully.

Prayer

Dear God,
We thank you for the individuality we enjoy, and for the freedom to grow in our own beliefs and values. Help us to live in peace and harmony, respecting the customs of others, caring for our fellow humans and not being blinded by the ignorance of racial, cultural or religious prejudices. Give us the courage to follow our beliefs, care for the future of the world and all who are in it and to share what we have with those less fortunate than ourselves.
Amen

Song   When I needed a neighbour   (Someone's Singing, Lord 35)

Common values

Hinduism

There is one God represented in many different ways and with different names.
It is important to care for all living creatures, and for the earth itself.
The family is very important – this includes grandparents, aunts, uncles, etc.
Honesty is highly valued.
Community worship occurs in a building known as a temple.

Sikhism

There is one God.
The Gurdwara is the name of the building where Sikhs gather to worship. It is also used as a meeting place for a variety of other functions.
Sikhs believe in the importance of working hard.
Family life is important.
All humans are equal and should be cared for.
Sharing with others (of any religion) is expected.
Truthfulness, tolerance and peace are important aspects of life.

Islam

There is one true God.
Great importance is placed on cleanliness, patience, prayer.
Honesty is highly valued.
The building where community worship takes place is called the Mosque.
Kindness and respect should be shown to guests.

Judaism

There is one God.
The family is important and special time is spent with the family on the Sabbath when no work is done.
Honesty is highly valued as is generosity.
The building in which Jews meet to worship is called the Synagogue.

Buddhism

Whilst Buddhists do not believe in God as a creator, they use statues and paintings of gods to help them to meditate.
The building for community worship is called a temple.
No other living creature should be harmed.
It is important to be generous to those who are in need.
You should never take more than you actually need.
No lies should be told, or hurtful remarks made to or about anyone.
Thoughtless or careless behaviour is not acceptable.

Christianity

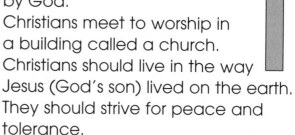

Everything was created by God.
Christians meet to worship in a building called a church.
Christians should live in the way Jesus (God's son) lived on the earth.
They should strive for peace and tolerance.
People should not strive for earthly riches, but should share what they have with those in need.
There is great importance placed on honesty, justice and caring for others.

Andrew Brodie: Assembly Today KS2 © A&C Black Publishers Ltd. 2005